The Little Book of Jokes for Kids of All Ages

D1146487

Zymurgy Publishing
The moral rights of author
Martin Ellis/Zymurgy
Publishing has been asserted,

All rights reserved. No part of this publication may be
reproduced, stored in a retrieval system, or transmitted in any
form or by any means without the prior written permission
of Zymurgy Publishing. Whilst every effort has been made to
ensure the accuracy of the facts contained in this publication,
no responsibility can be accepted by the author or Zymurgy
Publishing for errors or omissions or their consequences
A CIP catalogue record for this book is available from the
British library.

Printed in China by L.Rex
ISBN 978 1903506 31 8
Published by Zymurgy Publishing,
Newcastle upon Tyne
10 9 8 7 6
© Zymurgy Publishing 2012

Thanks to the following for helping with the jokes:

Malcolm Binks, Jack Burness, Charlie, Holly and Hope Calvert, Cam, Ian Davison, Anne Ellis, Jackie Farrant, Simon Gallagher, Lotte and Max Houghton, Sarah Hawkins, Steve Ingham, Lucy Jackman, Jenny Matthews, Iain and Stephen Megginson, Mike Mould, Abbie Murphy, Randall Northam, Jerry O' Shea, David and Michael Owen, Richard Ridley, Luke Robinson, Ron Wilcox, Y 6 pupils St. Columba's Wallsend and Ian Zabrocki.

I was reading a great book.

The history of glue, I couldn't put it down.

What do you call two banana skins on the carpet?

A pair of slippers.

Where do baby apes sleep?

In apricots.

What do you give a sick pig?

Oinkment.

How do monkeys make toast?

They put bread under a gorilla.

Doctor, Doctor, I think that I'm a dog.

For how long have you thought that you are a dog?

Since I was a puppy.

A customer went to a paper shop.

It had blown away.

W hy do squirrels swim on their backs?

To keep their nuts dry.

W hat do you call two robbers?

A pair of knickers.

My dog's got no nose

How does it smell?

Awful.

What do you call a Frenchman wearing sandals?

Fellipe Flop

A group of astronauts were planning a trip to the sun. They were asked if they were worried about the heat.

They said that it would not be a problem as they would go at night.

What do you call a dinosaur with only one eye?

Doyouthinkhesaurus.

What runs but never walks?
Water.

Did you pick your nose?
No, I was born with it.

Why did the hedgehog cross the road?

To see his flatmates.

What do you call a wobbly baby?

A jelly baby.

Knock, Knock,

Who's there?
Doctor.
Doctor Who?
How did you know?

What's brown and
sticky?

A stick.

How do you get 4 elephants in a mini?

2 in the back and 2 in the front.

How do you get 4 giraffes in a mini?

Don't be daft, giraffes won't fit in a mini!

What do you get if you cross a cat with a parrot?

A carrot.

What is the worst cat to have?

A catastrophe.

Which cheese is made backwards?

Edam.

Why do fire-fighters wear red braces?

To hold their trousers up.

Why do birds fly south?

Because it is too far to walk.

Doctor, Doctor – I think that I am invisible.

Next patient please.

Knock, knock who's there, who, who, who?

Is there an owl in there?

Doctor, doctor, I feel like a spoon?

Well sit down and don't stir.

What is a cat's favourite TV show?

The Evening Mews.

Why did the trumpet player put his trumpet in the fridge?

Because he wanted to play cool music.

What did one traffic light say to the other traffic light?

Please don't look, I'm changing.

Why do farts smell?

For the benefit of the deaf.

Doctor, Doctor, I think that I'm a pair of curtains.

Pull yourself together!

Doctor, every time I lift my arm above my head it hurts.

Don't hold your arm up then.

How does a penguin make pancakes?

With his flippers.

What's a penguin's favourite auntie?

Antarctica!

Did you hear about the cat that ate a ball of wool?

She had mittens.

Knock, knock, whose there?

Cows go.
Cows go who.
NO, cows go moo!

Where do cars go to play?

In a car park.

Why do we know cats aren't sensitive animals?

Because they never cry over spilt milk.

Doctor, doctor I think, I am turning into an orange.

Don't worry I can squeeze you in later.

What begins with T, ends in T and is full of T?

A teapot.

Doctor, doctor, every time I drink tea I get a pain in my eye.

Try taking the tea spoon out!

Two monkeys in the bath, one says oo–oo, ah–ah.

The other monkey says "Put some cold water in."

A packet of chipsticks are driving in their car and they see a packet of crisps walking along the road, so they stop and offer the crisps a lift.

The crisps say, 'No thanks, we're Walkers.'

Doctor Doctor I keep seeing double!

Take a seat.

Which one?

What did the fish say when it hit a wall?

Damn!

Is that prawn crackers?

No it just likes a good laugh.

Iwas putting up the Christmas tree and accidentally swallowed some decorations.

Next day I woke up with tinselitis!

What tells chicken jokes?

Comedyhens.

Doctor, doctor, I feel like a bucket.

Well you do look rather pale.

What do you call an aircraft which gives haircuts while the plane is moving?

British Hairways!

Why did the skeleton run up a tree?

Because the dog was looking for its bones.

Knock, knock.

Who's there
Scott.
Scott who?
Scott nothing to do with you.

Why did the beach blush?

Because the sea weed.

Knock, knock.

Who's there
Doris
Doris who
Doris locked, please let
me in!

What did the wave say
to the sea?

Nothing, it just waved.

What do you get when you cross a centipede with a parrot?

A walkie-talkie.

What do you call a pig that does karate?

Pork chops.

Did you hear about the scientist who built a time machine?

He made it tomorrow and is testing it last week.

What do you get when you cross a dinosaur with a pig?

Jurassic Pork!

Where do cows go on a Saturday night?

The mooooooooooovies.

Why did the lifeguard cross the road?

To get to the other slide!!

A horse walks into a bar.
The barman says why the long face?

A man walked into a corner shop.

He bought 4 corners.

What's the fastest cake?

A scone ....

A customer returned to the optician's with a pair of glasses that he had bought and complained that the glasses were useless.

He started to shout and upset the other customers, so the optician took him outside and asked him to look up at the sky.

The customer looked into the sky.

The optician asked the customer what he could see?

The customer replied,

"I can see the sun."
The optician said,
"93 million miles and you're complaining!"

A mummy polar bear and baby polar bear were stood next to each other.

The baby polar asks mummy polar bear if he is a polar bear.

Mummy polar bear tells baby polar bear, "Of course you are, your daddy is a polar bear, I am a polar bear, so you must be a polar bear.

So baby polar bear says,

"Why am I so cold?"

What do you call a polar bear in the desert?

Lost.

What's black and white and red all over?

A newspaper.

Who spends most time in the bathroom?

A plumber.

Why should you not do maths in a jungle?

Because if you add 4 and 4 together you will get ate.

Why couldn't the pony sing?

Because it was a little horse.

Doctor, Doctor, I feel like an apple.

We must get to the core of this.

What kind of coffee do vampires drink?

De-coffinated.

When is the time to go to the dentist?

2.30 (tooth-hurty)

Doctor, doctor, I feel like a dictionary.

I will have a word with you later.

Why was the nose
sad?

Because it wasn't picked.

What did the flag pole
say to the flag?

Nothing, it just waved.

What made the computer scream?

Someone stepped on the mouse.

What do you get if you cross a computer with a big dog?

A megabyte.

A man wanted a dog to take out for walks. He saw an advert for a dog that was described as well house trained, obedient, great with children and a good talker.

So he rang the owner up and arranged to meet the dog. When he called at the owner's house, he pointed out that in the advert it said good talker, and that must be mistake and surely he meant walker.

The owner told him that the dog was a great talker and he should ask the dog to tell him about himself.

So the man said hello to the dog and asked him to tell him about himself.

"Well." said the dog,

"My first job was with the police, not any old police dog. It was very exciting at first going on raids and chasing criminals, but I got tired of the early morning starts.

I then got a job as a mountain rescue dog. I spent my time in the countryside having a great time running all over the hills. It was mainly practice exercises looking for injured walkers, after a while I got bored as they always hid in the same place.

My last job was working for an Arabian sultan in the middle-east. I lived like a king, with an air conditioned kennel, a gold dog bowl and only the best steak to eat. But in the end I missed all my friends and Britain, so I decided to come home and have been with my present owner ever since.

"That's amazing," said the man, "I have never met a dog that has had such an interesting life and is able to talk. Why do you want to sell him?"

The owner said,

"I am sick of all his lies, fibs and tall stories."

What did one eye say to the other eye?

Something between us smells.

What did one toilet say to the other toilet?

Oh dear, you look a bit flushed.

What do you find in the middle of nowhere?

The letter 'h'.

How do you make a number one disappear?

Put a g in front of it and it is gone.

What has 2 hands but can not clap?

A clock.

How can you tell when a clock is hungry?

It will go back for seconds.

What do people do to naughty clocks?

They tick them off.

Why was the clock thrown out of the window?

To see time fly.

Why did the clock keep scratching itself?

Because it had ticks.

Why did the clock not work?

Because it needed a hand.

Why was the maths book unhappy?

It had far too many difficult problems.

What is the best thing about numbers?

You can count on them.

When are doctors angry?

When they run out of patients.

How do you fix a broken chimp?

With a monkey wrench.

How do you cut the sea in half?

With a seesaw.

Why are teddy bears never hungry?

Because they are always stuffed.

How do you turn soup into gold?

Add 24 carrots to it.

What is a sea monster's favourite meal?

Fish and ships.

Three children were playing in the park, they were about to go on the slide when a genie emerged and said,

"What ever you shout as you go down the slide, you will get a bucket of, but you must be original."

The first child rushed up the slide and screamed

gold as they went down the slide, then got a bucket of gold coins. The second child quickly followed and went down the slide screaming diamonds then got a bucket of diamonds.

The third child who never listened or paid attention, went down the slide and screamed weeee!

Why did the chicken cross the road?

To get to the other side.

Why did the skeleton not cross the busy road?

Because he lacked guts.

Doctor, doctor I think I am a kite.

Don't worry you will come down to earth later.

What falls but never gets hurt?

Rain.

Where do books
sleep?

Under their covers.

What do you call a
scared dinosaur?

A nervous rex.

Why were the middle ages so dark?

Because there were a lot of knights.

Why shouldn't you tell jokes if you are standing on ice?

Because it might crack up.

What goes oh, oh, oh?

Father Christmas
walking backwards.

What is a ghost's
favourite game?

Hide and shriek.

Why are hairdressers fast drivers?

Because they know all the shortcuts.

Where do sheep get their hair cut?

At the baa-baa shop.

What time is it when an elephant sits on your fence?

Time to get a new fence.

Why do elephants have trunks?

Well, they would look silly with suitcases.

Why did the teacher wear dark glasses?

Because she had a very bright class.

What is a cat's favourite colour?

Purr-ple.

Which vegetable should you not take on to a boat?

A leek.

Where do you take a poorly horse?

The horse-pital.

Why couldn't the bicycle stand up?

It was too tyred.

Why do elephants never forget anything?

Because nobody tells them anything in the first place.

Why did the banana go to the doctor?

It wasn't peeling well.

How many apples grow on an apple tree?

All of them.

Why do gorillas have huge nostrils?

Because they have big fingers.

Why did a child take a pencil to bed?

So that he could draw the curtains.

What do you call a monster that likes to dance?

Boogie Man

How does a monster like his eggs?

Terri–fried

There were 4 cats in a boat, 1 jumped out. How many were left?

None, they were all copycats.

Doctor, doctor, I feel like a yo-yo.

Sit down, sit down, sit down.

A patient goes to the doctor and says that he can't stop farting.

The patient says that they are silent and don't smell. The doctor writes out a prescription and tells the patient that the medicine will sort his nose out and asks him to come back next week to get his hearing checked.

Doctor, doctor, I feel like a camera.

I'll be with you in a flash.

Why did the cheetah never go on holiday?

Because it could never find the right spot.

How many knees do you have?

A right knee, a left knee and 2 kid-neys.

How many ears did cowboy Davey Crocket have?

A left ear, a right ear and a wild front-ear.

Why did the rooster cross the road?

To prove he wasn't a chicken.

Why did the man stare at the carton of orange juice?

Because it said concentrate.

What do you call someone who sits under a cow?

Pat.

Why was the nose tired?

Because it couldn't stop running.

Why did the skeleton
cross the road?

To get to the body shop.

Where did the skeleton
keep its jokes?

In its funny bone.

Knock, knock.

Who's there?
Banana.
Banana who?
Knock, knock?
Who's there?
Banana.
Banana who?
Knock, knock?
Who's there?
Orange.

Orange who?

Orange you are pleased that I didn't say banana again!

Knock, knock

Who's there?
No one.
Thank goodness.

What do you call a horse that travels around the world?

A globetrotter.

I thought my nose was bleeding but it's not.

What happens when the Queen burps?

She gets a Royal pardon.

When is a door not a door?

When it is a jar.

Doctor, doctor, I think that I'm a needle.

I can see the point.

What did one keyboard say to the other keyboard?

You're not my type.

Why couldn't the sailors play cards?

Because the captain stood on the deck.

Why did Tigger smell?

Because he played with Pooh.

Knock, knock.

Who's there?
Little old lady.
Little old lady who?
I didn't know you could yodel.

What do you call a sheep on a trampoline?

A woolly jumper.

What has a bottom on
its top?

A leg.

Why should you never
share a secret with a
clock?

Because time will tell.

Where do horses live?

In a neigh-bourhood.

What do you call a dinosaur with the runs?

A megasaurarse.

Why did the toilet roll, roll down the hill?

To get to the bottom.

Why do fish not like computers?

Because they are worried about getting caught in the internet.

What goes up but never goes down.

Age.

Knock, knock.

Who's there?
Pasture.
Pasture who?
Pasture bedtime.

What did the rug say to the floor?

I've got you covered.

A man walks into a bar.

Ouch!

How do cats do their shopping?

From a catalogue.

What do you call a Scotsman with halitosis?

MacBreath.

Why did the one-handed man cross the road?

To get to the second hand shop.

What do you call a
sleeping bull?

A bull-dozer.

What pet does
everyone have?

An arm – pet.

How did the chewing gum cross the road?

It was stuck to the chicken's claw.

How do you make milk shake?

Scare it.

Where do lions buy their clothes?

At jungle sales.

Why did the teacher turn on the lights?

Because the class were so dim.

Why did the tyre go on holiday?

Because it needed a break from the pressure.

What do you call a man with a car on his head?

Jack.

Which animal should you never play cards with?

A cheat – a.

Why are cooks cruel?

Because they beat eggs and whip cream.

What do you call a dog with no name?

You can't, he won't come.

What's yellow and makes a lot of noise?

Custard screams.

What did the mummy ghost say to the baby ghost that was eating its food too quickly?

Stop goblin.

What has eyes but can not see?

A potato.

A book never written:

Falling Off A Cliff

by Eileen Dover

A nother book never written.

Bubbles In The Bath
by Ivor Windy-Bottom

How did the egg climb up a mountain?

It scrambled up.

Why didn't the skeleton go to the party?

Because it had no-body to go with.

What did the doctor give the patient with a splitting headache?

A bottle of glue.

Two people were sat on a park bench, one says to the other, "Have you just farted?"

He replied, "Of course I have, you don't think I normally smell like this!"

Why are babies good at football?

Because they are natural dribblers.

Doctor, doctor, can you help me out?

Just return through the door that you came in through.

Knock, knock.

Who's there?
Boo.
Boo who?
No need to cry!

What has teeth but can not eat?

A comb.

What is the biggest wine at Christmas?

Children eating sprouts.

Thieves broke into a police station and stole the toilets.

A senior police officer said that they had nothing to go on.

What did one wall say to the other wall?

Meet me at the corner.

What dog is best at telling the time?

A watch dog.

What is the laziest mountain?

Ever – rest.

How did Noah light the ark?

With floodlights.

What's the difference between a TV and a newspaper?

Have you ever tried swatting a fly with a TV?

Why should you not tell jokes to an egg?

It might crack-up.

Where do frogs hang their coats?

In the croak–room.

Why are fish so clever?

Because they live in schools.

Why were the teacher's eyes crossed?

Because the class was so naughty.

How did Vikings send secret messages to each other?

By norse code.

What goes up and down but doesn't move?

Stairs.

Why did the lion spit out the clown?

Because he tasted funny.

Why can't dogs dance?

Because they have two left feet.

What did the farmer call the cow that had no milk?

An udder-failure.

What did the paper say to the pencil?

Write on!

What sound do hedgehogs make when they kiss?

Ouch!

What gets wetter the more it dries?

A towel.

Why is a fish so easy to weigh?

Because it has its own scales.

Why was the broom
late?

Because it over-swept.

What stays in the
corner but travels
the world?

A stamp.

Why did the poor dog chase its tail?

To make ends meet.

Where do polar bears vote?

At the north pole.

What is it that even the most careful person overlooks?

Her nose.

Why is Britain such a wet country?

Because the Queen has reigned for so many years.

What object is King of the Classroom?

The ruler.

What did the stamp say to the envelope?

Stick with me and we will go places.

What do you get from a pampered cow?

Spoiled milk.

Why did the music teacher have a ladder?

To reach the high notes.

What do horses wear to the beach?

Clip-clops.

Did you hear the joke about peanut butter?

I'm not telling you, you might spread it.

What do you get if you cross an elephant with a fish?

Swimming trunks.

What do pilots eat?

Plane biscuits.

What markets do dogs hate?

Flea markets.

What song is the favourite song for cats?

Three Blind Mice

What's got four legs
and one foot?

A bed.

Knock, knock.

Who's there?
Snot.
Snot who.
Snot nice to be left
outside.

A customer went into a bookshop and asked where the self-help section was.

She was told,

"I'm not telling you, it would defeat the purpose."

What's a pirate's favourite letter?

R.

What did the dentist say when a friend baked a cake?

Can I do the filling?